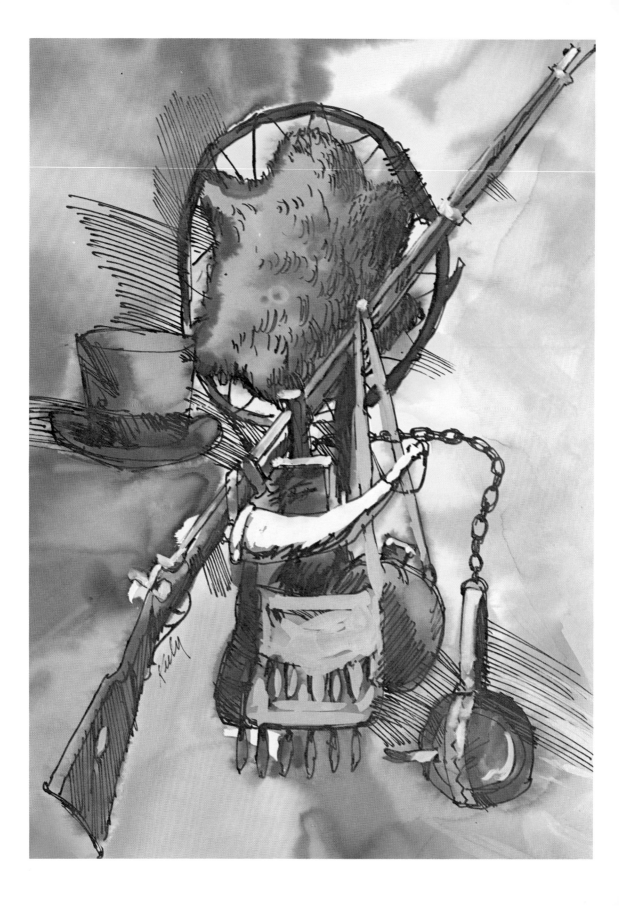

WE
THE PEOPLE
KIT CARSON

Published by Creative Education, Inc. 123 South
Broad Street, Mankato, Minnesota 56001

Library of Congress Cataloging-in-Publication Data

Zadra, Dan.
    Kit Carson : trailblazer of the West (1809-1868) / Dan Zadra ;
illustrated by John Keely and Dick Brude.

    p. cm. — (We the people)
    Summary: An easy-to-read biography of Kit Carson, who ran away
from home at the age of fifteen to begin a career as a hunter,
explorer, and mountain man.
    ISBN 0-88682-189-4
    1. Carson, Kit, 1809-1868—Juvenile literature.   2. Pioneers—West
(U.S.)—Biography—Juvenile literature.   3. Scouts and scouting—
West (U.S.)—Biography—Juvenile literature.   4. Soliders—West
(U.S.)—Biography—Juvenile literature.   5. West (U.S.)—Biography—
Juvenile literature.   [1. Carson, Kit, 1809-1868.   2. Pioneers.]
I. Keely, John, ill.   II. Brude, Dick, ill.   III. TItle.
IV. Series.
F592.C53Z33   1988
978'.02'0924—dc19
[B]   87-36384
[92]   CIP
                                                              AC

WE
THE PEOPLE
KIT CARSON

TRAILBLAZER OF THE WEST
(1809-1868)

DAN ZADRA

Illustrated By John Keely And Dick Brude

CREATIVE EDUCATION

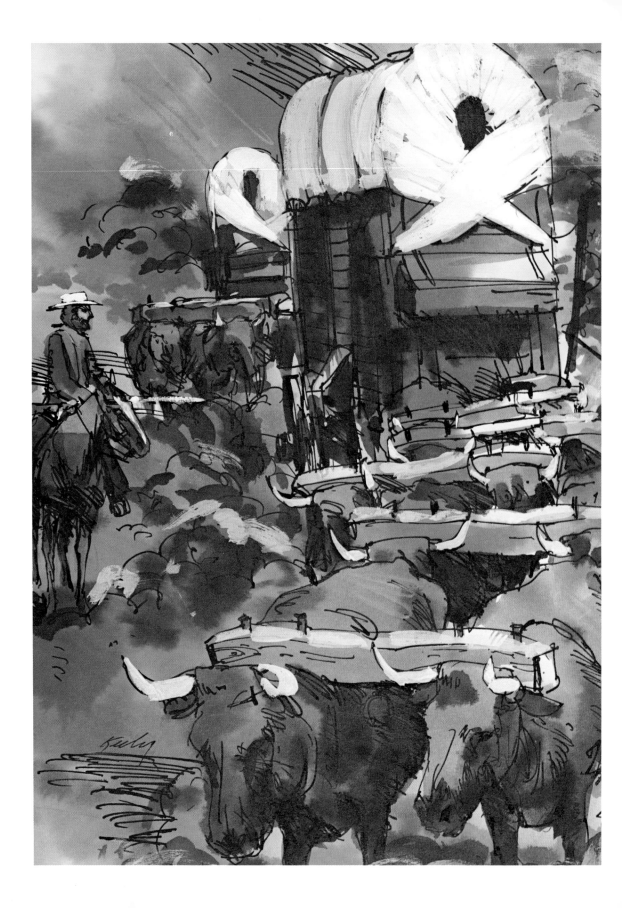

KIT CARSON

On a cloudy, wind-swept day in 1826, a boy watched a wagon train roll by. It was setting out on an 800-mile journey from Franklin, Missouri to Taos, New Mexico.

How he wished he could go along.
His name was Christopher Car-
son, but his friends called him Kit. He
was 16 and small for his age. His family had followed Daniel Boone to Mis-

souri from Kentucky. Then his father had died, and Kit's big, strong brothers had gone off to the Wild West. But Kit was the sheltered one. His mother said he would have to learn a trade—so he was apprenticed to a saddle-maker.

Kit hated the dull shop. Like his older brothers, he yearned for adventure. That night, he ran away—after the wagons.

He took an old mule, a twist of beef jerky, and his father's rifle. Before long, he met up with a party of hunters. They had no use for the boy—until Kit pulled out the old rifle and put on a shooting display. This "boy" could shoot like a man.

Kit learned to hunt and trap with the men. This was the life for him!

When they came off the trail at Santa Fe, New Mexico, someone showed Kit a Missouri newspaper. He read that the saddle-maker offered a one penny reward to anyone who would bring Kit Carson back to Missouri.

Kit just laughed. He knew he was free at last.

Over the next two years, Kit grew strong and tough. Odd jobs with wagon trains kept him fed. He still sat short in the saddle, but wiry muscles rippled beneath the colorful calico shirts he wore.

In 1829, he joined Ewing Young's beaver trappers. They had to fight the Indians and live outside in all kinds of weather. But Kit had never been happier. Naturally, when Young decided to go to California, Kit

wanted to tag along, too. He had no idea of the hardships he would encounter along the way.

Even in winter, the deserts they crossed were terrible. The men nearly died of thirst. They ate jackrabbits, sage hens, even rattlesnakes to survive. Finally they reached the green valleys of California. They stayed more than a year, trapping beaver. Then they returned to Taos, New Mexico, with valuable pelts.

Kit was 22 years old—no longer a fuzzy-cheeked boy but a seasoned trapper who had helped blaze a new trail to California.

In Taos, Kit took his first hot bath in months. He bought a warm meal and some new buckskins—and slept in a real bed at the hotel! He had sold

his beaver skins for a lot of money. But it did not last long in town. So off he went to the wilderness again. He joined another fur company and set out for the beaver country of the northern Rockies.

In those days, beaver fur was used mainly for fancy European hats. The trappers themselves were a wild bunch called "mountain men." They were among the first whites to explore the American Northwest—all in a day's work.

For seven years, Kit trapped throughout Wyoming, Idaho, and Oregon. He became known for his bravery and shrewdness. White explorers chose him to be their leader. The Indians honored him in legend and song. Kit fell in love with

an Arapaho maiden named Singing Grass. They married, and life was good.

Then, in the 1830's, the fashion for beaver hats ended. The mountain men had to find a new way of making a living. Kit took his band of men and his wife and baby to the garrison at

Fort Bent, Colorado. There he
formed a company that provided buffalo meat for the troops. Forty men
worked for him.

About the year 1840, Singing
Grass took sick and died. Kit worried
about his young daughter. How could
a grizzled old trapper like himself give

17

proper care to a little girl? Kit decided to take her to his sister in Missouri. On a riverboat outside St. Louis, he met a man who changed his life— John Charles Fremont.

Fremont was a young army engineer. He was in charge of an expedition going to map the first part of the Oregon Trail—between Missouri and the Rocky Mountains. Kit said:

"Let me guide you."

Fremont liked Kit Carson. People told him that this mountain man had traveled the western wilderness and knew it well. During the summer of 1842, the First Fremont Expedition explored Wyoming. It was during this trip that Kit's fame was assured. Fremont's men wrote a diary along the way—and Carson, their guide, was written up as the hero.

Kit returned to Taos and married Josefa Jaramillo, a young woman from a prominent family. She was his devoted wife for 25 years. They had seven children.

In 1843, Fremont mounted a second expedition. This one would last longer. They planned to explore

the lands west of the Rockies.
Fremont, of course, hired Kit Carson
to accompany him.

Fremont went along the Oregon
Trail in Wyoming. It was already
being traveled by settlers in wagons.
Then the expedition made a side-
trip, exploring the Great Salt Lake in
Utah. From there they went to the
Columbia River in Oregon—where
Kit Carson thought his journey

would end. But he had a surprise. They would turn south instead— into the unexplored Great Basin. Fremont hoped to find another river flowing westward.

They went south through the Oregon desert and into the arid badlands of northern Nevada. The country was nearly waterless. Both men and horses suffered terribly as they crossed barren lava plains and alkali flats.

The Carson Pass led them
westward over the High Sierra. Late
in February they arrived at Sutter's
Fort, California. The men were starv-
ing. The horses had eaten one
another's tails.

They rested, then went on. This
was country that Kit Carson had
traveled as a young man. The map
was still in his head. They crossed the

Mojave Desert in comfort this time. It was spring, a time of rain and flowers. They went into southern Nevada then marched easily northeast through Utah. A great curve took them back into Colorado, to good old Fort Bent. They had been gone a year and traveled 5,500 miles.

Fremont and his men wrote about this expedition, too. People all over the country came to admire Kit Carson. He was the best-known of the scouts and mountain men who helped to open the West.

Kit went on a third expedition with Fremont in 1845. This time they helped convince the people of California to rebel against Spanish rule. The war between Mexico and the United States began to rage.

During the war, Kit carried dispatches through enemy lines for Fremont and General Stephen Kearney. By the time the war was over in 1848, Mexico had been forced to give up California and most of its other lands in the Southwest. Kit Carson was invited to Washington where President Polk personally thanked him for risking his life for the

American cause.

With New Mexico now part of the United States, Kit thought he might become a simple rancher. But he decided that he probably couldn't put up with a tame life for long. Besides, there were still two more wars to fight!

Kit helped battle the fierce Apaches in the Indian uprisings of the mid-1800's. Later, he became an Indian agent and helped the red men

make peace with the government. It was a job he enjoyed. No man respected the Indian people more than Kit Carson.

When the Civil War broke out in 1861, he was among the first to volunteer for the Union. "Colonel" Cody commanded a regiment of volunteers and served with distinction.

Then the southwestern Indians began to make their final stand against the whites. Carson, now a brigadier general, was in the forefront of the Indian battles. He served as commander of Fort Garland in Colorado. There, in 1867, he was injured by a fall from a horse and never fully recovered. The adventurous mountain man whose action-packed life had helped tame the Wild West, died peacefully at home in 1868.

WE THE PEOPLE SERIES

WOMEN OF AMERICA

CLARA BARTON
JANE ADDAMS
ELIZABETH BLACKWELL
HARRIET TUBMAN
SUSAN B. ANTHONY
DOLLEY MADISON

INDIANS OF AMERICA

GERONIMO
CRAZY HORSE
CHIEF JOSEPH
PONTIAC
SQUANTO
OSCEOLA

FRONTIERSMEN OF AMERICA

DANIEL BOONE
BUFFALO BILL
JIM BRIDGER
FRANCIS MARION
DAVY CROCKETT
KIT CARSON

WAR HEROES OF AMERICA

JOHN PAUL JONES
PAUL REVERE
ROBERT E. LEE
ULYSSES S. GRANT
SAM HOUSTON
LAFAYETTE

EXPLORERS OF AMERICA

COLUMBUS
LEIF ERICSON
DeSOTO
LEWIS AND CLARK
CHAMPLAIN
CORONADO